Heather & Avery

And the
Magic Kite

Written By
Sharon
Deubreau

Illustrated By
Steve
Pileggi

Scriptor House LLC

2810 N Church St Wilmington, Delaware, 19802

www.scriptorhouse.com

Phone: +1302-205-2043

Published by Scriptor House LLC

Paperback ISBN: 979-8-88692-054-3

eBook ISBN: 979-8-88692-055-0

Heather and Avery are cousins.

Heather is 6.
She likes her fish Swimmy,
everything purple, and playing with Avery.

Avery is 4.
He likes balls, trucks, and playing with Heather.

Heather and Avery are best friends.

One sunny and breezy spring day,
Heather and Avery went to fly kites,
but in the garage there was only one kite.

Instead of sharing like best friends,
they grabbed the kite at the same time.

All of a sudden, in a WHOOSH and a whirl....

Heather and Avery were standing in a field.
It was no longer sunny.
Scary dark clouds were everywhere
and the nice breeze became a strong howling wind.

In the field they saw a man flying a kite.
He was a rather strange looking fellow.

He was old, and his long white hair
was blowing about his head.

He wore a frilly white shirt over his chubby belly,
a long brown coat, and teeny gold glasses.

The strange man looked away from his kite to see
Heather and Avery watching him.

He called to them to come closer.
Keeping their eyes fixed on his kite, they did.

The kite was high in the sky, waving wildly
as if begging to come out of the clouds.

Then it started to rain, and the man asked
Heather and Avery,
"What are you children doing out here in this weather?"

"We wanted to fly our kite, but…
where are we?" replied Heather.

"Philadelphia, of course.
I'm sorry, I should introduce myself.
I am Mr. Franklin.
What are your names?"

"I am Heather and he is Avery."

"My Daddy says not to fly kites in the rain,"
Avery insisted.

"Well, he is right, Avery.
But today I am trying an experiment."

"What's an experiment?" asked Avery.

"An experiment is something like a test."
explained Mr. Franklin.

"I don't like tests." said Heather.

"This is not that kind of test," Mr. Franklin chuckled.

"Have you ever watched lightning during a storm?"
Mr. Franklin continued.

"It's scary," said Avery.

"Well, it can be scary because it is very powerful,"
Mr. Franklin told them.

"So why are you flying that kite in a storm?" Heather asked.

"Do you see that metal key on the kite string?"
asked Mr. Franklin

"Yes," they both chimed.

"This kite will get that key close to the lightening, and I
want to see if the lightning passes through the key."

"What does it mean if it does, Mr. Franklin?"
asked Avery.

"Let's just wait and see,"
Mr. Franklin replied.

Then, with a crack and a boom,
lightning hit the kite.

All of a sudden the key began to glow!

"Yes, YES! Do you see that, children?

This means that lightning is really a stream of
electrified air.
Just imagine the possibilities!"

"So," Heather began,
"Are you saying electricity is in the air?"

"I am not sure it is as simple as that, Heather."

"Well, why don't you just turn on the light for electricity?"
Avery asked.

"Turn on the light?. . ."
started Mr. Franklin.

Then, in a whirl and a WHOOSH...
Mr. Franklin was gone and
Heather and Avery were in the garage, holding their kite.

It was raining and the
wind whipped the leaves around.

"Let's find a key!" said Avery.

"No, Avery. We are not supposed to fly kites in the rain."

They put the kite away and ran into the house.

Dodging raindrops, they never realized
that they had witnessed a piece of history.

FIFTEEN FAST FACTS

Benjamin Franklin

1706	Born in Boston January 17
1718	Went to work for his brother James, a printer
1722	Became a vegetarian (so he could save money and buy more books)
1730	Opened "The Library Company", the first lending library in the country
1732	Published Poor Richard's Almanack
1736	Organized the Union Fire Company fire department
1741	Published one of America's first magazines
1752	Conducted kite experiment
1762	Mapped Postal routes in the colonies
1764	Charted Gulf Stream
1776	Served on a committee of five who draft the Declaration of Independence
1783	Signed Peace Treaty w/England
1784	Invented bifocals
1786	Invented the instrument for taking down books from a shelf
1790	Died in Philadelphia April 17, at the age of 84